Castrato

Winner of the 1992 Canadian National Playwriting Award, Greg Nelson is a dedicated writer whose plays have been produced across western Canada and in England. After the critical success of his first full length play, *Sydney*, Greg Nelson's *Castrato* secures his position as both an innovative and crafted playwright. With many fringe and radio productions behind him, Greg Nelson's dramatic insight is a developed and cultivated tool, evident both in the pace and readability of *Castrato*.

Greg Nelson lives and writes in Edmonton.

Castrato

a play by
GREG NELSON

Blizzard Publishing • Winnipeg

Castrato first published 1993 by
Blizzard Publishing Inc.
301–89 Princess St., Winnipeg, Canada R3B 1K6
© 1993 Greg Nelson

Cover design by Scott Barham.
Printed in Canada by Printcor.

Published with the assistance of
the Canada Council and the Manitoba Arts Council.

Caution

This play is fully protected under the copyright laws of Canada and all other countries of the Copyright Union and is subject to royalty. Except in the case of brief passages quoted in a review of this book, no part of this publication (including cover design) may be reproduced or transmitted in any form, by any means, electronic or mechanical, including recording, and information storage and retrieval systems, without permission in writing from the publisher, or, in the case of photocopying or other reprographic copying, without a licence from Canadian Reprography Collective (CANCOPY).
 Rights to produce, in whole or part, by any group, amateur or professional, are retained by the author.

Canadian Cataloguing in Publication Data

Nelson, Greg, 1965–
 Castrato
 A play.
 ISBN 0-921368-31-3
I. Title.
PS8577.E47C3 1993   C812'.54   C93-098065-4
PR9199.3.N44C3 1993

To my parents, for their goodness.

Playwright's Note

An image came up during one of the workshops at Theatre Network. We were talking about lighting—how light and shadow work as representations of good and evil.

And the image was this: a person, who endeavours to stand in the light, must necessarily cast a shadow. In fact, the light is invisible until it strikes a person. It is the act, the endeavour to stand in a moral place, which reflects the light ... but which also creates the shadow.

And the tidy moral we extracted from this was: it is better to cast a shadow than to stand in the dark.

Castrato premièred at Theatre Network's NEWrites Festival, Edmonton, on February 19, 1993, with the following cast:

PETER	James MacDonald
STERN	Wendell Smith
STEPHEN	Greg Lawson
LINDA	Jan Alexandra Smith

Directed by Stephen Heatley
Set Design by Judith Bowden
Lighting Design by Ruth Lysak-Martynkiw
Costume Design by Nola Augustson
Stage Managed by Betty Hushlak

Castrato was workshopped by Theatre Network, the Saskatchewan Playwrights Centre, and Theatre B.C. It was dramaturged, at various times, by: Stephen Heatley, D.D. Kugler, Conni Massing, Kim McCaw, Jan Selman, Patti Shedden and Roy Surette. In 1992, *Castrato* won Theatre B.C.'s Canadian National Playwriting Competition.

The Playwright gratefully acknowledges the assistance of the 1991 Banff Centre for the Arts Playwrights' Colony and the Wallace Stegner House in Eastend, Saskatchewan.

Special thanks to Jan Selman, Stephen Heatley, and Patti Shedden for their support.

Characters

PETER: Reverend Peter Maclean, 28. Protestant.
STEPHEN: Stephen Maclean, 30. Businessman.
STERN: Reverend Jonathan Stern, 60. Minister at St. Andrew's Church.
LINDA: Linda Clark, late twenties. A radio journalist.

Setting

Edmonton. Present.

Act One

Scene One

(Lights up on PETER, preaching in Hoover. He reads from a text.)

PETER: Exhibit A: The Holy Bible. Our guiding light. The source of our so-called Christian Morality. If the Bible's for a thing, that thing is *right*. If the Bible's against a thing, that thing is *wrong*. Isn't that how it goes?

Exhibit B: a notebook. My father's diary. The pages contain his favourite Bible verses, snipped out of the Holy Book with a pair of scissors and fastened to the pages of this notebook with glue.

I'm going to tell you a Bible story.

(He stares at his congregation.)

Twelve years ago my father, the Reverend Harold Maclean, preached a sermon in which he said, and I quote, "I am castrated. You have castrated me." And then my father went home, and he took a bath, and he slashed his wrists, and he died. But before he died he made one final entry in his diary. It was taken from the book of Romans chapter eight verse thirteen. And it read: "If by the Spirit you put to death the deeds of the flesh you will live."

(He pauses.)

I haven't told you about my father, have I. He was a bastard. A first class son of a bitch. Overflowing with violence and hatred. From the pulpit he spewed poison down upon his congregation. And at home he spewed abuse upon his children. And he used, as a weapon, the verses of the Bible. Verses taken not from *this* book ... *(Holds up Bible.)* but from *this* book. *(Holds up diary.)*

Tell me. How many of you are keeping diaries? How many of you are abusing your children? How many of you are using the Bible as a weapon to promote violence and hatred? Come on. Let's see a show of hands.

Scene Two

(The office of Reverend Jonathan Stern, at St. Andrew's. STERN is at his desk, speaking on the phone. STEPHEN enters. STERN waves him in, motions him to sit down.)

STERN: Great! Well that sounds just great Bob, I had no idea ... uh huh ... uh huh ... well that's just great ... I will, you bet I will ... okay Bob, keep me posted ... Bye for now. *(Hangs up.)* That was Bob.

STEPHEN: Good news?

STERN: He's just about to sign a deal with a station in Calgary.

STEPHEN: You're kidding.

STERN: I'm not kid—

STEPHEN: Calgary!

STERN: Apparently they liked my tape.

STEPHEN: That's great!

STERN: I don't quite believe it myself. Things are moving very quickly.

STEPHEN: So they should.

STERN: And I have you to thank for it Stephen.

STEPHEN: No—

STERN: Yes I do. You introduced me to Bob. You set the wheels in motion.

STEPHEN: All I did was make a few calls.

STERN: I tell you this thing has got *momentum*. I mean with this deal I can reach the entire *province*.

STEPHEN: Incredible.

STERN: There is a greater power at work here. Behind this project.

STEPHEN: Yes.

STERN: I feel that God is with us.

(Pause.)

So. How are you Stephen you look sick.

STEPHEN: I'm fine.

STERN: Are you sure? You look terrible.

STEPHEN: I've just been traveling too much, you know, hotel beds.

STERN: You haven't been sleeping?

STEPHEN: Yeah, but it's no big deal.

STERN: Stephen—

STEPHEN: I'm fine—

STERN: Have you been—

STEPHEN: I'm *fine* Jonathan, *really*. Hey, listen, I hear you preached a real humdinger on Sunday.

STERN: Well ...

STEPHEN: I'm sorry I missed it, I, I was delayed. I barely made it back in time for the committee meeting. They said you were brilliant.

STERN: Did they?

STEPHEN: They *raved* about it.

STERN: I'm afraid I got carried away.

STEPHEN: Sounds to me like you outdid yourself.

STERN: It went well.

STEPHEN: Really?

STERN: Yes. In fact it went extremely well. I wish you could have been there, Stephen. It was one of those moments of ... transcendence. I can hardly remember what I said. I mean I didn't even *look* at my notes.

STEPHEN: Wow.

STERN: I felt that I was an instrument. A direct pipeline. You know? Like Mozart. It was marvelous.

STEPHEN: You're going to be a tough act to follow Jonathan.

STERN: Well ...

STEPHEN: No, I mean it, you are. No matter *who* we get.

STERN: Well, it's about time I moved on if you ask me. St. Andrew's needs a change.

STEPHEN: Not true.

STERN: Now. Tell me about the meeting.

STEPHEN: *(Pause.)* Well, it was short. I did most of the talking.

STERN: Uh huh.

STEPHEN: First thing I did was bring up your guy, George Evans.

STERN: Good.

STEPHEN: I said that you had personally recommended him, that you were old friends, that he was a good man.

STERN: And ...?

STEPHEN: Well, they were easily convinced.

STERN: Excellent.

STEPHEN: They were ready to hire him sight unseen.

STERN: No no, do it by the book. Bring him in, have him preach a sermon or two, *then* offer him the job. We're breaking enough rules as it is.

STEPHEN: Well, actually—

STERN: I hope we can keep this quiet Stephen, my involvement I mean. I hope that you and the committee understand that.

STEPHEN: Of course we do.

STERN: Because although it's not entirely ethical—

STEPHEN: *(Overlapping.)* Well—

STERN: —it is necessary.

STEPHEN: I know.

STERN: We have to make the right choice Stephen. This is a critical time for the entire church, this issue is threatening to split it apart.

STEPHEN: I know.

STERN: We need someone like George Evans, someone solid, someone dependable.

STEPHEN: Well, actually, that wasn't the end of the meeting.

STERN: *(Pause.)* What do you mean.

STEPHEN: I, uh, I brought up another name. Another candidate.

STERN: What?

STEPHEN: I didn't have time to speak to you first, so I just went ahead—

STERN: What other candidate?

STEPHEN: *(Pause.)* I was talking to Harold Brown last week. You know Harold.

STERN: Yes.

STEPHEN: Well he's a client. And he came into the office last Monday and he told me about his weekend. He'd been visiting his in-laws in a little town south-west of here called Hoover. And they went to church. And the minister there was a man named Peter Maclean and was he any relation.

STERN: Peter?

STEPHEN: And I thought, no way, it's impossible. But all week I had this *feeling*, so I said to hell with it I have to know for sure. So I drove down. On Sunday morning. And it was him.

STERN: Your brother.

STEPHEN: Yes. I hadn't seen him since he was sixteen. And now he's twenty-eight and a minister. I mean, how could he possibly be a minister?

STERN: Did you speak to him?

(No response.)

Stephen?

STEPHEN: No. I couldn't. I panicked. When I saw him, when I, when I looked at him up there in that pulpit, when I heard his voice, I, I started to sweat, and, and feel sick, you know, to my *stomach*.

STERN: All right ...

STEPHEN: *(Angry.)* I thought I was *finished* with those feelings Jonathan, I thought I had *dealt* with them.

STERN: All right Stephen, just, listen to me, those feelings are perfectly natural. It is *okay* to be upset. We've talked about this.

STEPHEN: I know.

STERN: You were angry with your father, for killing himself, you were full of anger and rage and fear and that is why you left.

STEPHEN: That's right.

STERN: And because you abandoned your little brother, because you *deserted* him, you felt a terrible guilt.

STEPHEN: Yes.

STERN: A terrible, terrible guilt. For leaving him alone.

STEPHEN: Yes.

STERN: And now you've seen him again, for the first time, of *course* those feelings are going to come back.

STEPHEN: That's right.

STERN: Of *course* they are. It's perfectly *natural*. And you can deal with them. As long as you remember ...

STEPHEN: I know.

STERN: ... that you are a good man.

STEPHEN: Yes.

STERN: Who deserves to be forgiven.

STEPHEN: Yes.

STERN: We are all of us good men, Stephen, every one of us, and we all deserve to be forgiven.

STEPHEN: Every one of us.

STERN: Including your father. And including your brother. And including you. *(Pause.)* God loves you Stephen. And He forgives you. Remember: in Christ we are redeemed. In Christ we need not doubt, nor fear, nor tremble. *(Pause.)* We knew this was going to happen. Didn't we.

(STEPHEN nods.)

We knew that Peter was bound to turn up sooner or later. And now he has, and that's okay, and we can deal with it. Right?

STEPHEN: I'd like him to be considered. For St. Andrew's.

STERN: What?

STEPHEN: I'd like him to come up and preach a sermon or two. And then I'd like to give him the job.

(Pause.)

STERN: Well now let's just think about this.

STEPHEN: I have thought about it.

STERN: How long has he been ordained.

STEPHEN: I don't know.

STERN: Not very long, he's twenty-eight.

STEPHEN: So?

STERN: So, St. Andrew's is a big city church, it, it requires someone responsible—

STEPHEN: I know.

STERN: Someone *mature*. How do you know he can handle it?

STEPHEN: I don't.

STERN: How do you know he's got the right ideas?

STEPHEN: Well—

STERN: Where does he stand on The Issue?

STEPHEN: He's with us.

STERN: Are you sure?

STEPHEN: Look, Jonathan, I just want to give him a chance. He deserves a chance. And so do I.

STERN: Of course you do.

STEPHEN: I've been dealing with these feelings of, of ...

STERN: Guilt.

STEPHEN: ... of guilt for long enough.

STERN: Of course you have. Look, I know what you've been through, Stephen, I *know*. And that is why I want to be *careful*. I want to be sure that you are ready to deal with this. *(Pause.)* I really wish you'd spoken to me first. Before you took it to the committee.

STEPHEN: I know. I'm sorry.

STERN: What exactly did you tell them?

STEPHEN: I said he was bright, young, smart, full of energy.

STERN: I see. And what was their response?

STEPHEN: Well, they were easily convinced.

STERN: I see. *(Pause.)* All right. Okay. Let's give him a chance.

STEPHEN: Okay.

STERN: Who knows, he might be just the thing we need, a burst of *energy*.

STEPHEN: That's right.

STERN: Someone to carry on where I leave off.

STEPHEN: Exactly.

STERN: But ... let's go slow.

STEPHEN: Yes.

STERN: Let's make sure it's the best thing for *you*.

STEPHEN: Right.

STERN: I'm mostly concerned about *you*. *(Pause.)* Now. Why don't we have a prayer. Would you like that?

STEPHEN: Yes. Jonathan?

STERN: Yes Stephen.
STEPHEN: Thank you.

Scene Three

(The sanctuary of St. Andrew's. PETER enters. He stands and looks up at the cross.

LINDA enters from the opposite direction. She carries a tape recorder over her shoulder.)

LINDA: Excuse me.

PETER: Hello.

LINDA: You don't work here do you.

PETER: Well, not—

LINDA: Does anybody work here?

PETER: Well—

LINDA: I have an appointment with Reverend Stern.

PETER: I think he went for lunch.

LINDA: Lunch?

PETER: Yes.

LINDA: Of course he did. I've been trying to do this interview for a week, and every time we make an appointment he doesn't show up. I'm starting to think he's avoiding me. Or is that just paranoia?

PETER: *(Extending hand.)* Hi. I'm Peter Maclean.

LINDA: Hi. Linda Clark. This is not a good day. I shouldn't have got out of bed this morning, that was my first mistake.

PETER: Linda Clark.

LINDA: I'm a reporter, I work for—

PETER: For the CBC.

LINDA: That's right.

PETER: CBC Radio. The morning show.

LINDA: Right.

PETER: I've heard your stuff. I think you're very good.

LINDA: *(Beat.)* You do?

PETER: Yes. In fact you're the only reason I listen.

LINDA: Really.

PETER: I'm afraid I find the rest of the show pretty dull. Sorry.

LINDA: No, don't be sorry.

PETER: Of course it's still better than anything *else* on the radio, but, frankly, not by much. I mean it seems to be designed to put people to sleep, don't you think?

LINDA: Well—

PETER: To convince them not to worry about anything, to just walk around with stupid smiles, you know, *stunned*. I mean God forbid that anyone should think, or, or have an idea or actually say something original.

LINDA: Well—

PETER: I just think it's boring and stale. Sorry—

LINDA: *(Overlapping.)* That's—

PETER: —I'm not trying to be rude.

LINDA: That's all right. I agree with you.

PETER: What?

LINDA: Completely.

PETER: You do?

LINDA: Yes, actually, I do.

PETER: *(Pause.)* That's why I like your stuff. It makes me think.

LINDA: Well. Good.

(Pause.)

PETER: So. You're here for an interview.

LINDA: That's right. It's for a new series I'm doing on morality.

PETER: Oh?

LINDA: Yes, with a capital "M". What do we consider right and wrong, where do we *get* these ideas ...

PETER: Really.

LINDA: I know, it's a ridiculously broad topic.

PETER: No, it's good.

LINDA: And so of course I thought of Reverend Stern.

PETER: Why "of course"?

LINDA: What?

PETER: Why Reverend Stern?

LINDA: *(Pause.)* Are you a member here? At St. Andrews?

PETER: No. I'm from out of town.

LINDA: How far out of town.

PETER: A little place called Hoover. You've never heard of it.

LINDA: So you don't know about Stern.

PETER: Well actually—

LINDA: He tends to be very outspoken, you know, he likes to take up *positions*. He just came out against gay clergy, which is *the* big moral issue in the church—

PETER: Yes, I know.

LINDA: Right, well, he's against it. He's also against abortion, birth control, pre-marital sex, you name it. I figure he's just to the right of the *Pope*. I mean according to Stern, women should stay home and have babies and cook dinner for their husbands, God, I mean he's still living in 1953! And you know, the amazing thing is, he always has a Bible verse to back him up. *Always.* It's incredible. You're not a friend of his are you?

PETER: No.

LINDA: Good. So, what, you're just ... visiting?

PETER: Actually, I'm here to preach a sermon.

LINDA: What?

PETER: On Sunday. Are you aware that Stern is leaving St. Andrew's?

LINDA: Yes.

PETER: Well, apparently I'm a potential successor.

LINDA: *(Pause.)* You're a minister too?

PETER: Yes.

LINDA: Really?

PETER: Yes.

LINDA: Oh. Listen, I didn't realize, I, I wasn't *knocking* Stern—

PETER: You weren't?

LINDA: No, I was just—

PETER: Why not, *I'd* knock him, he sounds like a dreadful man.

LINDA: *(Pause. Smiles.)* Well he is. Dreadful. Which is why he'd be a good interview.

PETER: *(Smiles.)* Right. Of course.

LINDA: Aren't you supposed to wear one of those little white collars?
PETER: I don't think so.
LINDA: I mean you don't look like a minister, you look ...
PETER: Interesting?
LINDA: Normal.
PETER: Well, thank you. I think.
LINDA: So you do know about Stern.
PETER: Yes.
LINDA: And you disagree with him.
PETER: Completely.
LINDA: So how could you be his successor?
PETER: That's a very good question. *(Pause.)* Sounds interesting, doesn't it.
LINDA: Yes.
PETER: Sounds like a good story.
LINDA: What was your name again?
PETER: Peter Maclean.
LINDA: Tell me something, Reverend Maclean. What if I were to ask about *your* views on morality.
PETER: Well—
LINDA: Would you actually say something original?
PETER: *(Smiles.)* Tell you what. Why don't you come to church on Sunday.
LINDA: Okay.
PETER: I'll give it my best shot.

Scene Four

(Stephen's office in a downtown skyscraper. Big windows. STEPHEN calls to PETER.)

STEPHEN: Peter! Over here.
PETER: Hi. This place is confusing.
STEPHEN: Yeah, I figure they built it that way on purpose. *(Laughs.)* Come in, come in.
PETER: Hello Stephen.

(STEPHEN embraces PETER, awkwardly.)

STEPHEN: It's good to see you. Sit down. Would you like a drink?

PETER: No. Thanks.

STEPHEN: Okay. Cigarette?

PETER: I don't smoke.

STEPHEN: Good for you. I've been trying to quit, but I just can't find the time I guess. So. This is where I work.

PETER: It's quite the building.

STEPHEN: Nothing like this in Hoover I'll bet. Check out the view.

PETER: Wow.

STEPHEN: Look over there. Right there. See that tiny little steeple there?

PETER: Uh huh.

STEPHEN: That's the church. That's St. Andrew's. Looks pretty small from up here, doesn't it.

PETER: Tiny.

STEPHEN: Yeah.

(Pause.)

How's the hotel.

PETER: Good, fine.

STEPHEN: Comfortable?

PETER: Very comfortable.

STEPHEN: Good. Good.

(Pause.)

PETER: So what do you do exactly.

STEPHEN: Real estate.

PETER: Ah.

STEPHEN: Yeah, office towers, plazas, that sort of thing.

PETER: Right.

STEPHEN: Lot of pressure, lot of traveling, but, you know ... I love it.

PETER: Did you go to school?

STEPHEN: For a while, yeah, yeah. You?

PETER: Yes.

STEPHEN: Of course you did. Bible school.

PETER: In Winnipeg.

STEPHEN: Really! Hey, great town, Winnipeg. *(Pause.)* So you, uh, you're not married?

PETER: No.

STEPHEN: Me neither. Well, I was—I'm divorced. It ... it was a mess, you know, I was too young, we only lasted a couple of years.

PETER: How young.

STEPHEN: Eighteen. Her name was Janet. Still is, I guess.

PETER: I remember Janet.

STEPHEN: You do? Right. Of course you do. *(Pause.)* You know Peter I ... uh, I tried to find you. Several times. I never could. Did you try to find me?

PETER: No.

    (Pause.)

So.

STEPHEN: Right.

PETER: Can we start at the beginning? I'm a little confused.

STEPHEN: Of course you are.

PETER: You said on the phone that you would explain when I got here.

STEPHEN: Well—

PETER: Your call came completely out of the blue.

STEPHEN: Yeah—

PETER: How did you find me?

STEPHEN: Well, one of my clients has family in Hoover.

PETER: Uh huh.

STEPHEN: And he told me about you. And so I went down.

PETER: What?

STEPHEN: I didn't tell you.

PETER: You were in Hoover?

STEPHEN: Yes.

PETER: When.

STEPHEN: Sunday morning. I sat at the back.

PETER: That was you.

STEPHEN: Did you see me?

PETER: Yes. *(In explanation.)* The way they built the church, the way the window is, the sun shines directly in my face and I can't really see the congregation. I could see somebody sitting back there but I didn't know who it was. I spent the whole service trying to figure out who it was because he looked *familiar*, he looked like ...

STEPHEN: Like who.

PETER: Like ... our father. I looked for him after the service, but he was gone, I mean I thought it was a *ghost*.

STEPHEN: Right.

PETER: I mean because I was *preaching* about him—

STEPHEN: Right.

PETER: Why didn't you stay?

STEPHEN: I know—

PETER: You should have—

STEPHEN: I *know*, I should have Peter, you're right, I know, I ... but I just ... I didn't have time.

PETER: Oh. *(Pause.)* And now suddenly I'm up for St. Andrew's.

STEPHEN: Yes. And I intend to make sure you get it.

PETER: Things aren't suppose to happen this quickly Stephen.

STEPHEN: Well, we took a few shortcuts.

PETER: There should be a committee—

STEPHEN: There *is* a committee, Peter, and I'm *on* the committee.

PETER: I see.

STEPHEN: And that's why you're here.

PETER: And the next two weeks are like a try-out.

STEPHEN: It's just a formality, really. They're gonna love you.

PETER: How do you know.

STEPHEN: I know. Look, let me worry about the committee, okay? You just do your thing.

PETER: That's the problem.

STEPHEN: What.

PETER: My thing. It's not very popular. Hoover is in a state of shock. And it likely won't go down too well at St. Andrew's either.

STEPHEN: Of course it will.
PETER: No, Stephen, I'm not like Reverend Stern, I'm different.
STEPHEN: Look—
PETER: Very different.
STEPHEN: Good! That's what we *want*. Somebody *new*, somebody young, fresh, *different*, someone with lots of *energy*.
PETER: Well—
STEPHEN: This is a major opportunity for you, Peter, a big promotion, I mean St. Andrew's is a big city church—
PETER: I know—
STEPHEN: You'd be crazy not to want this job.
PETER: Of course I *want* it, I'm just warning you—
STEPHEN: *(Irritated.)* All right then good! That's all that matters, you want it, it's yours! I can make it happen! Okay? That's what I'm saying! *(Pause.)* I'm going to have a cigarette. Will it bother you?
PETER: No. Go ahead.

(STEPHEN takes a pack of cigarettes and an ashtray from his desk drawer. He lights a cigarette, inhales deeply. PETER watches him.)

STEPHEN: They're going to *love* you here Peter, I know they are. The *congregation* is going to love you, the *committee* is going to love you, *Stern* is going to love you. Hey, I've seen you preach and you are good. Really good.

(No response from PETER.
STEPHEN smokes.)

Listen. About your sermon. On Sunday, the one I saw.
PETER: What about it.
STEPHEN: It was good.
PETER: Thank you.
STEPHEN: You were preaching about …
PETER: Our father.
STEPHEN: Right, and you … you had a diary.
PETER: Yes.
STEPHEN: Is it for real?
PETER: Yes.

STEPHEN: I thought it didn't exist. I thought the papers made it up.
PETER: It does. They didn't.
STEPHEN: How long have you had it?
PETER: Twelve years.
STEPHEN: How did you get it?
PETER: I found it. It was right beside him. On the toilet seat.
STEPHEN: Oh. *(Pause.)* I never saw it.
PETER: I know.
STEPHEN: Why didn't I see it?
PETER: Because I didn't show it to you. And then you left. Remember? With Janet.
STEPHEN: Yes. I remember. *(Pause.)* I'd like to read it. Can I read it?
PETER: Of course.
STEPHEN: Thank you.

(Pause. STEPHEN smokes.)

You know Peter, I … frankly I think you may have gone a bit overboard. In your sermon.
PETER: Oh?
STEPHEN: I mean you made him sound like some kind of monster, you kept talking about *abuse*. What were you referring to, I don't remember any abuse.
PETER: What?
STEPHEN: I mean *yes* he was troubled and, and he was a strict disciplinarian, but he was still a good man, wouldn't you say?

(No response from PETER.)

I think you may have a distorted view of things Peter. You were pretty young when he died, and it was a very traumatic time, for both of us, very traumatic—
PETER: *(Interrupting.)* No, I *wouldn't* say our father was a good man.
STEPHEN: Really.
PETER: *(Calm, fluid.)* I would say he was an evil man. I would say he was a drunkard and a bully who abused his children and lived a public life of almost total hypocrisy.
STEPHEN: *(Pause.)* Well. That sounds familiar.
PETER: What do you mean.

STEPHEN: I used to think that way too. Exactly the same, I was full of anger and rage and ... and guilt. But then something happened. Something that allowed me to forgive my father, to see that he was in fact a good man.

PETER: What happened.

STEPHEN: I went to church. And I heard Jonathan Stern.

(Pause.)

He was preaching a sermon on forgiveness. And I sat there, and I listened to him preach, and I realized right there and then that I needed to *talk* about this. I needed to deal with my anger, and my rage, and my guilt, so I did. I went to him. And I talked to him. And he showed me how to forgive. And I know Peter that he is there for you. If you need him. If you need to ... talk.

PETER: *(Pause.)* Well. Thank you Stephen. I'll certainly keep that in mind.

(Stephen's phone buzzes. STEPHEN answers it.)

STEPHEN: Yes. Oh, yes, good, send him in. *(Hangs up.)* Well speak of the devil, perfect timing.

PETER: What do you mean.

STEPHEN: *(Hides cigarettes and ashtray in desk.)* Jonathan's here. He mentioned he was coming downtown so I told him to stop by and meet you.

(STERN enters.)

Jonathan, hello, come in, come in.

STERN: Hello Stephen, I can't stay, I'm on my way to a meeting.

STEPHEN: No problem, listen, Jonathan, I'd like to introduce you to my brother, Reverend Peter Maclean. Peter, Reverend Jonathan Stern.

PETER: *(Shaking hands.)* Hello.

STERN: Well, I'm pleased to finally meet you Peter. I've heard a lot about you.

PETER: Oh?

STERN: Welcome to town.

PETER: Thank you.

STEPHEN: Can you believe it, I haven't seen this guy for twelve years! *(Laughs.)*

STERN: *(To PETER.)* Stephen assures me you're full of enthusiasm.

STEPHEN: Absolutely.

PETER: Well, I—

STERN: I'm looking forward to hearing you preach. I'm curious to see if you're anything like your father was. I heard him a number of times. Excellent preacher.

PETER: Well I think you'll find—

STERN: A tragic story, Peter, tragic. Your father was a good man, a very good man.

PETER: You think so?

STERN: Yes. And I want you to know that I understand what you've been through. Don't I Stephen.

STEPHEN: That's right.

STERN: I understand. *(Pause.)* Now. I want to ask you something Peter and I hope you won't take offense. Around here we like to call a spade a spade, and, after all, these are tricky times. We have to be careful.

PETER: Of course.

STERN: Tell me. Are you ... are you married Peter?

PETER: No, actually, I'm not.

STERN: I see. Any specific reason?

PETER: No, nothing specific.

STERN: I see. You just, uh ...

PETER: Sorry?

STERN: I mean it's not because you're, you know, in any way, uh ...

STEPHEN: Of course he isn't Jonathan.

STERN: Right, right. Good. Well. I just want to be absolutely clear.

STEPHEN: Of course.

STERN: There's no point mincing words. I mean frankly, the last thing St. Andrew's needs or wants is one of *those* in the pulpit. We don't want *that* much of a change!

   (STERN laughs. STEPHEN does too.)

   (To PETER.) You understand. *(To both.)* Well listen, I'd love to stay and chat, but, my producer waits.

PETER: Your producer?

STEPHEN: Jonathan's working on an exciting new project.

STERN: Television.

PETER: Really.

STERN: It's a whole new world, Peter, you wouldn't believe it. Very exciting.

PETER: I can imagine.

STERN: *(Shaking PETER's hand.)* Good to meet you Peter. Have you been by the church yet?

PETER: Yes, they gave me an office to use.

STERN: Good, good. Well. See you on Sunday. Take care Stephen.

STEPHEN: You too Jonathan.

(STERN exits. STEPHEN calls after him.)
Have a good meeting! *(To PETER.)* He's a wonderful man. He's been like a ... you know. He likes you. I can tell.

PETER: I feel like I've just been initiated.

STEPHEN: What?

PETER: Into a club.

STEPHEN: What do you mean.

PETER: Why did he want to meet me?

STEPHEN: Well, he—

PETER: What exactly is his role in this.

STEPHEN: *(Beat.)* He doesn't have one.

PETER: Really?

STEPHEN: Peter—

PETER: Because if he does—

STEPHEN: Peter, come on, it's his church for crying out loud, he's *interested*, that's *it*.

PETER: I hope so.

STEPHEN: Hey! Relax! This is going to work out! I know it won't be easy, none of this is easy, but we have to give it a chance, right? Come on, let's just ... make it happen.

PETER: *(Pause.)* Okay.

STEPHEN: All right. That's better. I mean let's not forget we're brothers, right, we're *family*.

PETER: Right.

STEPHEN: I mean have we got some catching up to do! Twelve years! God!

PETER: Look—

STEPHEN: Twelve years!

PETER: Look, I'm sorry Stephen, but I'd like to keep this on a business level. For now anyway.

STEPHEN: What?

PETER: This isn't about us. Or our past. It's business.

STEPHEN: But—

PETER: All right? Business. Nothing more.

STEPHEN: *(Pause.)* All right Peter. If that's what you want.

PETER: When is the interview?

STEPHEN: The what?

PETER: With the committee.

STEPHEN: Oh. Uh, not until next weekend. After your second sermon.

PETER: Great. Well I should go. You've got work to do.

STEPHEN: Yeah, okay. *(Pause.)* Well, I guess I'll see you on Sunday then. At church.

PETER: Great. See you then. *(Pause.)* Bye.

(PETER turns, begins to leave.)

STEPHEN: Peter. *(PETER stops.)* Just one thing. In your sermon this Sunday?

PETER: Yes.

STEPHEN: Just ... don't come on too strong. Okay? I mean the committee's gonna love you, I know they are but, just ... you don't wanna scare anyone off. Right?

(No response.)

Right Peter?

Scene Five

(PETER, preaching at St. Andrew's. He is dressed in his robes. He reads from a written text. He preaches with confidence.)

PETER: "To set the mind on the flesh is death, but to set the mind on the Spirit is life and peace ... for if you live according to the flesh, you will die; but if by the Spirit you put to death the deeds of the flesh, you will live."

"If by the Spirit you put to death the deeds of the flesh, you will live."

From the book of Romans, Chapter Eight, verses six and thirteen. A passage that I am rather too familiar with. You see, it was the text of my father's suicide note.

Some of you will remember my father. He was the minister that slit his wrists. The minister with the famous diary that supposedly described his frequent visits to prostitutes. Remember? It was in all the papers.

But I'm not going to talk about my father this morning. I want, instead, to talk about the Bible. About that passage from Romans, about spirit and flesh.

(He pauses.)

During the seventeenth and eighteenth centuries in Europe there flourished a kind of operatic rock star, known as the Castrato. Young boys were castrated before puberty. Their voices kept their soprano range, and, as the boys grew they attained the most powerful, most malleable voices ever heard. They were described as "perfect," "not-human," "not of this world."

The first castrations were done by the church for the benefit of the Pope's private choir. And this is where it gets creepy. The *reason* they were castrated was because The Bible, in some obscure passage, states: "Women must be silent in the churches." And since silence precluded singing, the Castrati were created to fill the gap. Secondly, the *justification* for the castrations was also The Bible, in fact it was an equally obscure passage from ... Romans: "If by the Spirit you put to death the deeds of the flesh, you will live."

The church claimed to be enhancing the spirits of the Castrati by liberating them of their flesh, by putting it to death, and the ultimate *proof* of this enhancement was the astounding *beauty* of the castrated voice. In short, brutal acts of violence were done in the name of God. And in the name of The Bible.

It's time I made my point.

My point is that Romans was wrong. The Bible was wrong. And the church was wrong. Mutilating young boys is no way to praise God.

My point is that flesh and spirit must not be separated. Putting flesh to death in the name of spirit and life and *beauty* is utter nonsense. It is when flesh and spirit come *together* that true beauty exists, the beauty that ennobles, the beauty that is humanity, the beauty that was Jesus Christ: "And the word was made flesh." Christ who saw beauty in everyone, regardless of shape or size. Regardless of sex. Regardless of occupation. Regardless of health. Regardless of ... regardless of ... marital status. That is my point.

We must be careful how *we* praise God. Are we committing acts of violence? Are we denying flesh in the name of an inhuman spirit? In the name of some obscure Biblical passage? Are we denying Jesus Christ?

We must put an end to our castrations. We must uphold *true* beauty. The beauty of spirit *and* flesh.

Because, if we don't, we will end up like the church of the seventeenth century, and, indeed, like my father ... with blood on our hands.

Let us pray.

Scene Six

(Peter's office at St. Andrew's after the sermon. PETER removes his robes. LINDA enters.)

LINDA: That was great.

PETER: Hi. You came.

LINDA: That was an excellent sermon.

PETER: Well—

LINDA: It was, it was concise, provocative—

PETER: Thank—

LINDA: *Resonant*—

PETER: Thank you.

LINDA: It made me *think,* it was like a breath of fresh air. I've been coming to hear Stern, you know because of the interview.

PETER: Right.

LINDA: Do you realize you just contradicted everything he's been saying? Not that anybody noticed—I doubt that they got it.

PETER: Really?

LINDA: Have you ever heard Stern preach?

PETER: No.

LINDA: They're used to something a little simpler. Stern doesn't ask people to think.

PETER: Right.

LINDA: He likes to do their thinking for them.

PETER: What has he been saying?

LINDA: Well, basically that if we allow gays in the pulpit we'll all get AIDS. Which would be God's punishment and serve us all right.

PETER: *(Delighted.)* Of course!

LINDA: Well not in those exact words but that was the gist of it. So you can imagine how you sounded in comparison, I mean you used a *metaphor*, my *God!*

PETER: Yeah.

LINDA: *Very* radical.

PETER: I shouldn't have held back.

LINDA: What do you mean.

PETER: I chickened out, at the last moment, I changed the wording.

LINDA: What wording.

PETER: "Sexual orientation." I changed it to "marital status." Which sounded just ... lame.

LINDA: Why did you chicken out?

PETER: Because I have to take it easy. If I want the job.

LINDA: And you seriously think they're going to hire you?

PETER: That's what my brother tells me.

LINDA: Who's your brother.

PETER: The chairman of the search committee.

LINDA: Oh. Right. So that's how it works.

PETER: That's how it works.

(Pause.)

LINDA: It *was* about your father, wasn't it.

PETER: What?

LINDA: The sermon. You said you weren't talking about your father but I think you were.

PETER: Really.

LINDA: I've been doing some research. Harold Maclean. It *was* big news, it got national coverage. The sermon he preached, the one about being castrated. The suicide. The *diary*. Is this okay? Can I talk about this?

PETER: Go ahead.

LINDA: You don't mind?

PETER: I don't mind.

LINDA: Well ... the thing is ... it's a great story. Not just your father, *you*. All of this happens, and you become a minister. *Why?*

PETER: Right.

LINDA: And then I come here this morning, and not only are you preaching about castration, you're preaching about *morality*.

PETER: Right, with a capital "M".

LINDA: I mean, I don't want to sound flip, so if I'm pushing it, tell me.

PETER: Okay.

LINDA: It's just ... you're a great story.

PETER: Well. Thank you.

LINDA: You're welcome.

(They smile.)

So why *did* you become a minister.

PETER: That's a big question.

LINDA: Okay—

PETER: With a big answer.

LINDA: Okay, why did your father say he was castrated.

PETER: *(Beat.)* I don't know.

LINDA: I'm pushing it aren't I.

PETER: No.

LINDA: Yes I am. Sorry. I noticed you were reading your sermon. From a text.

PETER: Yes.

LINDA: Do you always write them out? You never just improvise?

PETER: Not any more. I get myself in trouble.

LINDA: What kind of trouble.

PETER: Well ... the church I'm at now. In Hoover. I think my days are numbered.

LINDA: Why. What did you do.

PETER: I told them ... I ...

LINDA: *(Smiling.) What?*

PETER: I told them they were fucking hypocrites.

LINDA: Really?

PETER: Yeah. And that they were full of shit.

LINDA: *(Delighted.)* You're kidding!

PETER: Well they *were*.

LINDA: You said that in a sermon?

PETER: I was trying to make a point! No, I wasn't, I was trying to shock them, I admit it. I was just sick and tired of hearing them *snoring* all through the service. I was sick of seeing my words bouncing off them and falling on the floor and being muffled by this thick layer of dust that covers everything. I wanted to bash a hole in the ceiling, I wanted to smack them. I wanted to get one word, just one word into their heads. And I did. Unfortunately it was the wrong word.

LINDA: No kidding.

PETER: They just make me so angry. And when they do wake up, when they do read the Bible, they just pervert it, they use it to justify their hatred, their small-mindedness.

LINDA: Sounds like a dreadful place.

PETER: It is.

LINDA: Sounds a lot like St. Andrew's. I mean this church is no different. Shouldn't you find one that you agree with?

PETER: No, that's just it, that's the whole point, I want this one. Because I believe that I can repair the damage Stern has done. That I can restore thought, that ... that I can wash his poison off the fucking walls. Maybe that's crazy.

LINDA: No, it's not, no way. It's admirable.

PETER: And as long as I keep to my text ... maybe I can actually do it.

LINDA: Do you want my advice?

PETER: Sure.

LINDA: My advice is, get the job.

(Pause.)
What are you doing tonight. Do you have any plans?
PETER: No. Why.
LINDA: Well, I'd like to talk to you some more ...
PETER: Okay.
LINDA: And maybe I could buy you dinner.
PETER: *(Beat.)* Great.
LINDA: Where are you staying. I'll pick you up.
PETER: The Westin.
LINDA: Seven o'clock?
PETER: Okay.
LINDA: Great. See you then.
   (LINDA exits. PETER looks after her.
   STEPHEN and STERN enter.)
STEPHEN: There he is, the man of the hour.
PETER: Hello Stephen. Reverend Stern.
STERN: Hi Peter, I only have a moment.
STEPHEN: Hey. That was a great sermon.
PETER: Thank you.
STEPHEN: Terrific. Really made me think.
STERN: I agree. You've got talent Peter. Lot of ideas.
STEPHEN: Good ideas.
PETER: Thank you.
STERN: Tell me. Do you always preach from a text?
PETER: Yes.
STERN: I've never been able to do it myself. Tried it a couple of times, but I only lasted a page or two and then I ignored it completely. *(Chuckles.)* Chucked it!
   (STERN laughs. So does STEPHEN.)
I like to speak from the heart, not from the page.
STEPHEN: *(To PETER.)* It's true. Right from the heart.
STERN: You should try it Peter. I know I know, you don't want to make a fool of yourself, but I'll tell you something. The only way you'll

ever *really* communicate with people is by looking 'em right in the eye. Huh? Not looking down at a page.

STEPHEN: Good point.

STERN: God has made us ministers not of the letter, but of the spirit—

PETER: Well—

STERN: "For the letter killeth but the spirit giveth life."

PETER: Actually—

STERN: I feel I should be frank Peter. The fact is, you were full of ideas this morning, but you simply weren't *communicating*. I mean, what were you actually *saying?* I couldn't figure it out. Could you Stephen?

STEPHEN: Well, I uh—

STERN: Stephen couldn't figure it out. Nobody could, Peter, that was the problem.

PETER: Well—

STERN: I mean you have to be concrete. You have to give your congregation something to chew on, something they can *grasp,* you have to deal with an *issue*—

PETER: I did deal with an issue.

STERN: Well, I don't think you did Peter, I—

PETER: Well then perhaps you weren't listening.

STERN: *(Beat.)* I beg your pardon?

STEPHEN: Peter—

PETER: I do communicate.

STERN: Well now—

PETER: I'm not melodramatic, and I don't manipulate emotion, but I *do* communicate. I simply ask people to think.

(Pause.)

STEPHEN: *(To STERN.)* I don't think Peter's saying—

STERN: That's all right Stephen. I understand what Peter is saying. *(Pause.)* How old are you Peter? Twenty-two, twenty-three?

PETER: Twenty-eight.

STERN: And how long have you been a minister?

PETER: One year.

STERN: One year. Tell me. What made you follow in your father's footsteps? I mean it's rather an odd choice considering your past.

PETER: Well—

STERN: You didn't like your father did you Peter.

PETER: What?

STERN: You believe that he was wrong, that his *ministry* was wrong, that everything he did and said and *stood* for was wrong.

PETER: Look—

STERN: And you are taking it upon yourself to do it right. Your father preached from the heart, so you will preach from the page. Your father was passionate, so you will not be. It's too bad your father died before you could see your error. Before you could learn to *forgive* him, to see that he was a good man, a good preacher—

PETER: That's—

STERN: Just, let me finish Peter. Let me say that maybe you aren't fighting him at all. Maybe what you are fighting is the anger, the *rage* that you still feel inside you. And let me say Peter that it is a fight you cannot win. Not until you come face to face with the fact that your father is not your foe. Your *anger,* your *rage—that* is your foe. *(Pause.)* And it is not a battle you can fight alone. You need help. I am willing to give you that help. Stephen is willing.

STEPHEN: That's right.

STERN: All you need to do … is reach out your hand. "Let not your heart be troubled: ye believe in God, believe also in me."

(Pause. PETER says nothing.)

STEPHEN: That stuff's not easy to hear Jonathan.

STERN: I know it isn't.

STEPHEN: I'm sure Peter needs some time, to, uh …

STERN: Of course.

STEPHEN: Why don't you tell him your ideas for the show.

STERN: All right.

STEPHEN: *(To PETER.)* Jonathan would like to get you involved.

STERN: Well let's just say the possibility exists. Assuming we can see eye to eye.

STEPHEN: Of course you will.

STERN: *(To PETER.)* Stephen seems to think you'd be an asset.

STEPHEN: That's right.

STERN: And I would like to maintain a close connection with St. Andrew's. Maybe even do some filming here.

STEPHEN: Why not, it's a great location.

STERN: The whole project is very dynamic. Believe it or not, I'm modeling the show on Johnny Carson, I was a big fan of his.

STEPHEN: Great show.

STERN: So. Start with a big intro, something stirring but familiar like uh, *(He sings, STEPHEN joins in.)* "Who would true valour see / Let him come hither." Then, out I come and it's right into a bit of sermon. Nothing too long, but direct, you know, from the heart, very upbeat, very exciting. Prove to the average viewer that religion is *not* boring and stuffy, it's dynamic, *meaningful* ...

STEPHEN: Get them back into the churches where they belong.

STERN: I mean, why aren't young people going to church?

STEPHEN: Because they're watching TV.

STERN: Because they're watching TV. Okay. So we have to get right into their televisions.

STEPHEN: That's right.

STERN: We have to help these kids make the right *choices* Peter, I mean the stuff that's out there now—

PETER: *(Interrupting.)* What sort of choices?

STERN: Well, choices which will lead to a healthy and moral lifestyle.

STEPHEN: A Christian lifestyle.

PETER: A heterosexual lifestyle.

STERN: Yes. Precisely. Now—

PETER: What if I told you that I think the Bible is bullshit.

STERN: *(Pause.)* I beg your pardon.

STEPHEN: What?

PETER: Bullshit. I think the Bible is bullshit. Would you still want me on your show?

STEPHEN: *(To STERN.)* I think Peter just needs a little time—

STERN: The Bible—

PETER: Genesis nineteen, one to eleven.

STERN: Pardon?

PETER: *(Rapidly.)* Leviticus eighteen, twenty-two. Leviticus twenty, thirteen. First Corinthians six, nine to eleven. First Timothy one, one to ten. Romans one, twenty-six to twenty-seven. Bullshit. And that is just the beginning.

STERN: I see.

STEPHEN: *(To PETER.)* Peter you don't mean that.

PETER: *(Calmly, to STERN.)* I want nothing to do with you Reverend Stern. Or your show. Nothing.

(Pause.)

STERN: I see. Well. I'm sorry for wasting your time.

STEPHEN: Jonathan—

STERN: Excuse me.

(STERN exits.)

STEPHEN: *(After him.)* Jonathan, wait ... *(To PETER.)* What is the *matter* with you, how could you be so *rude?*

PETER: I wasn't rude, I was succinct. He was trying to manipulate me.

STEPHEN: He was trying to *help* you.

PETER: Bullshit.

STEPHEN: He is a wise and pious man—

PETER: Oh come on—

STEPHEN: Who has been in ministry for thirty-five years and deserves your respect!

PETER: Look, this is your fault Stephen—

STEPHEN: *My* fault?

PETER: I *told* you I didn't agree with him, I *told* you I was different—

STEPHEN: It's not my fault you insulted him—

PETER: And you said great, different is great, that's what we want, you said you could get me the job—

STEPHEN: I *can* get you the job.

PETER: *(Overlapping.)* So what does *Stern* have to do with it? It's not his decision it's the committee's decision—

STEPHEN: I know—

PETER: What does Stern have to do with *anything?* I mean he seems to think he knows all about me and my past and my innermost feelings about my dead father. God, he's got this entire bullshit *theory* worked out which you have obviously swallowed—

STEPHEN: Jonathan has done nothing but help me Peter, he saved my life.

PETER: What does that mean.

STEPHEN: I would have been dead by now. He saved my life.

PETER: Stephen, I don't know what that *means*.

STEPHEN: It means I was dying! I was trying to kill myself! I was full of hatred and fear and self-loathing, and I was walking onto the bridge. And I was climbing onto the rail. And I was preparing to jump into the dark waters—

PETER: Whoa, look—

STEPHEN: And Jonathan stopped me, Peter. He reached out his hand. But it wasn't only his hand it was Christ's hand too. And together they pulled me off that rail, they *saved* me. And you know how they did it? By showing me how to forgive my father, by showing me that he was a good person. And when I forgave him Peter, I also forgave myself. And I saw that I was good too. I saw that I was a good person, Peter, that I was *good*. That I was *good! (Pause.)* And from that moment on it was simple. From that moment on I took control of my life, I just did it. And now I am alive. Because I met Jonathan Stern. And I met Jesus Christ. And I can't help thinking Peter that maybe you should meet them too.

PETER: The Good One.

STEPHEN: What?

PETER: The Good One, you were always the Good One. Remember?

STEPHEN: No.

PETER: You don't remember?

STEPHEN: *No.*

PETER: You're kidding.

STEPHEN: Remember what?

(Pause.)

PETER: Tell me something. What did you forgive him *for?*

STEPHEN: Our father?

PETER: Yes.

STEPHEN: For dying. For the suicide.

PETER: And yourself?

STEPHEN: *(Pause.)* I forgave myself for leaving. Because I should have stayed with you. But I didn't. I abandoned you.

(Pause.)

PETER: *(Suddenly businesslike.)* You're right, Stephen, I *was* rude to Reverend Stern. I made a mistake and I apologize. All right? And although I appreciate that you have a relationship with him, I don't want any part of it. I don't want to be "helped." I don't want to be told that I am good. And I don't want to forgive anyone.

STEPHEN: Well—

PETER: *But.* I do want this job. So. Let's follow the proper procedure. All right? Let's not deal with Stern. Let's deal with the committee.

STEPHEN: *(Pause.)* All right.

PETER: Thank you.

(PETER gives STEPHEN the notebook.)

Here. I brought you this.

STEPHEN: What.

PETER: The diary. You said you wanted to read it.

STEPHEN: Oh. Yes. I do. Thank you.

PETER: Perhaps it will refresh your memory.

Scene Seven

(Peter's hotel room. PETER and LINDA enter, in the middle of a discussion. They are slightly drunk.)

LINDA: That's not what I'm saying, that's not—

PETER: *(Overlapping.)* That *is* what you're saying—

LINDA: —what I'm saying, no it *isn't*—

PETER: So what are you saying?

LINDA: *(Laughing.)* What I'm *saying* is, what I'm, what I'm *saying*—

PETER: Uh huh—

LINDA: What I'm *saying* is, I still contribute, I mean I'm as much a part of the problem as, you know …

PETER: Johnny Carson?

LINDA: *Johnny Carson* is, exactly, thank-you. Was.

PETER: That's not true—

LINDA: Yes it is. I mean, obviously we're on a totally different scale and he was in *television,* but essentially we're the same—

PETER: No—

LINDA: Yes we are because we are both part of mediums which only want to entertain. *Yes* we are giving information, *yes* we are asking questions, but we are forced to be entertaining—

PETER: But—

LINDA: *Yes,* which ultimately trivializes both the content and ourselves because we are thus pandering to an oppressive patriarchy which is also entrenched in, in ... in our mediums.

PETER: *(Beat.)* Wow.

LINDA: So there.

PETER: I think you just won the argument.

LINDA: It's like what you were saying this morning. In your sermon.

PETER: It is?

LINDA: Yeah. Sort of.

PETER: Well then I agree. *(Pause.)* So. Here it is.

LINDA: Yeah.

PETER: Pretty fancy, huh?

LINDA: Very fancy.

PETER: The bathtub has a whirlpool.

LINDA: Would you like some wine?

PETER: Good idea. I'll call room service.

LINDA: Not necessary. I have a bottle in my bag.

PETER: You're kidding.

LINDA. *(Rummaging.)* Always be prepared. One bottle of wine and one corkscrew.

PETER: That's great.

LINDA: Do you have any glasses?

PETER: Yes. In the bathroom. Don't move.

(PETER exits to bathroom. LINDA opens wine.)

PETER: *(Off.)* So why are you doing it?

LINDA: What?

PETER: *(Off.)* If you hate your job why are you doing it?

LINDA: I don't hate my job, I hate the network.

PETER: *(Off.)* Right.

LINDA: I mean, don't you hate the church?

(PETER enters with two small glasses. LINDA pours.)

PETER: Good point.

LINDA: So why are you a minister?

PETER: Yeah.

LINDA: Because you want to repair the damage. Well so do I. I'm *sick* of interviewing people like Stern.

PETER: I thought you said he'd be good.

LINDA: Not good. Loud.

PETER: Right.

LINDA: I want to interview someone who knows how to think. And talk. Like you.

PETER: Well—

LINDA: Not that I'm trying to flatter you. I'm not. Okay I am. *(Pause.)* You're not the minister type.

PETER: No?

LINDA: No. If you were lined up with three other people and somebody said which one is a minister, I wouldn't pick you.

PETER: Neither would I. *(Pause.)* I'll be honest. I'm not crazy about interviews. When I was sixteen, when my father died, the reporters kept asking me questions.

LINDA: Yes, I read the coverage. You were "The Traumatized Teenage Son."

PETER: Right. And they asked me why he had said that in his last sermon. About being castrated, they asked me what that meant.

LINDA: Right.

PETER: And I ... I lied to them. I told them about the diary. And I told them it said he went to prostitutes.

LINDA: That was a lie?

PETER: Yes. I made it up. *(Pause.)* You asked me today why I became a minister. Do you still want to know?

LINDA: Yes.

PETER: Okay. *(Pause. Calmly.)* When I was born my mother died. In childbirth. And my father blamed me for her death. He never said "you killed her," he didn't put it that way, he put it in terms of himself, in terms of his grief. His pain. He blamed me for his pain. He said that I had castrated him.

And apparently the only way he could ease this pain was by giving it back to me. So he did. In spades. He filled my life with pain.

He used to say that I was the Bad One. Stephen was the Good One; and I was the Bad One. You see because I had castrated him, and Stephen hadn't. And so everything that Stephen did was right. And everything that I did was wrong. He was incredibly consistent.

LINDA: That's obscene.

PETER: And so, when the reporters asked me what he meant, I didn't want to tell them. So I made something up. Something sensational.

LINDA: You should have told them the truth. It's much worse.

PETER: They didn't want the truth.

LINDA: Right.

PETER: Besides. The truth was none of their business.

LINDA: You must have hated him.

PETER: No, I hated Stephen.

LINDA: What about your father?

PETER: No, I didn't hate my father. I was afraid of him, but I didn't hate him. *(Pause.)* Do you believe in evil? I'm serious. Do you believe that there are evil people?

LINDA: I don't know.

PETER: I do. People who are dark inside. And you can always tell who they are, because they inspire fear. And that is the source of their power. And they have a lot of power.

LINDA: Fear.

PETER: Yes. Fear is the rational response to evil. *(Pause.)* My father was an evil man.

I used to have a lot of nightmares. After he died I used to dream about him. And I would wake up screaming. Night after night. I would scream and scream.

And then I got older and although I still had the nightmares, I managed to stop screaming. I was able, when the fear rushed over me, to stand it, somehow. And eventually I understood how it was that I could stand it, eventually I was able to put a name on it, and the name was God. God, for me, was the strength to not wake up screaming.

And I became a minister. And I began to fight my father's God, a God of fear. And to speak of my God ... a God of strength. And eventually, I stopped having the nightmares.

(He pauses.)

But you know, sometimes, when I'm preaching, the fear comes back. Very strong. And there I am, somehow reading out the words that I have written, and all the time the fear is rising up inside me. Like a scream. And I ask myself, why am I afraid? Where is the evil?

(Pause.)

God. Listen to me. I'm sorry.

LINDA: No—

PETER: I shouldn't have got started on this. I'm sure you're fascinated—

LINDA: No—

PETER: Aren't *I* a fun date.

LINDA: No, it *is* fascinating, it's, really, and not just because it's research, I mean not that it *is* research, it *isn't,* it's—

PETER: I'm starting to babble.

LINDA: No you're not.

PETER: I get carried away sometimes—

LINDA: You aren't babbling.

PETER: I just—

LINDA: Peter, you're being very clear.

(Pause.)

Would you like some more wine?

PETER: Sure. *(LINDA pours.)* Thank you.

(Pause.)

So.

LINDA: So.

PETER: Any more questions?

LINDA: No. Not tonight.

PETER: Good.

(Pause.)
LINDA: This isn't exactly a professional situation, is it?
PETER: Not exactly.
LINDA: I would even call it unprofessional.
PETER: So would I.
(They kiss.)
LINDA: This is not …
PETER: I know.
LINDA: I shouldn't be doing this.
PETER: Me neither.
(They kiss again.)

Scene Eight

(STEPHEN, alone, sleeping. The diary is in front of him. He is having a nightmare.)
STEPHEN: *No!*
(He sits up, terrified.)
I'm … not … *good!*
(Blackout.
End of Act One.)

Act Two

Scene One

(Stern's office. STEPHEN sits, waiting for STERN. He is exhausted. STERN enters, STEPHEN stands.)

STEPHEN: Jonathan.

STERN: I only have a moment Stephen.

STEPHEN: No problem.

STERN: I'm glad you dropped by. I wanted a word with you.

STEPHEN: Me too. I, I've been trying to get in touch with you.

STERN: Yes.

STEPHEN: Since Sunday. You haven't been in.

STERN: No, I haven't. I was in Calgary.

STEPHEN: Really?

STERN: Yes, I had several days of meetings there, I just got back this morning. Please. Sit down.

STEPHEN: *(Sitting.)* Meetings about the show?

STERN: That's right.

STEPHEN: Listen, Jonathan, I've been thinking about this TV thing.

STERN: Oh?

STEPHEN: Yeah, and I, I think maybe I can help in a more concrete way. Set up a few meetings myself, you know, talk it up a bit downtown, see if I can drum up some sponsorship.

STERN: Well, that's very kind of you Stephen, I'll pass that on to Bob. I'm not actually involved in the financial side.

STEPHEN: Oh.

STERN: I try to keep out of it. I'm purely creative on this project, I'm concentrating on the *ideas.*

STEPHEN: Right, right, of course. Good for you.

(Pause.)

STERN: So. This brother of yours.

STEPHEN: Right. Well—

STERN: I've been giving the matter some serious thought.

STEPHEN: Me too.

STERN: Frankly, I'm concerned.

STEPHEN: You're upset, I understand.

STERN: I'm not upset, I'm concerned. He made it clear the other day that he does not have a responsible attitude towards the Bible *or* ministry.

STEPHEN: Well—

STERN: He's too unpredictable, too wild.

STEPHEN: Well I'm concerned too Jonathan, *very* concerned, I ... and I spoke to him, and, uh, he ... he asked me to apologize.

STERN: Mm hm.

STEPHEN: He's, he's still very young, Jonathan, you know, very *fresh,* and, and *passionate,* it's ... he just has to *steer* that passion in the right direction.

STERN: Stephen. I'm afraid he has to go.

STEPHEN: What?

STERN: I said we'd give him a chance and we did and, as it turns out, he's simply not ready.

STEPHEN: But—

STERN: I think you'd better talk to the committee. And then perhaps you should get in touch with George Evans.

(Pause.)

STEPHEN: Look, let's give it another week. Okay? We'll hear another sermon and *then* we'll make a final decision.

STERN: No. I'm sorry Stephen. I will not allow Peter to preach at St. Andrew's again.

STEPHEN: *(Pause.)* We agreed that he would preach two sermons.

STERN: Yes—

STEPHEN: Not one.
STERN: I'm aware of—
STEPHEN: I think he deserves another chance.
STERN: Not right now he doesn't. Perhaps when he's had a chance to mature—
STEPHEN: It's not your decision.
STERN: What?
STEPHEN: It's the committee's decision. Not yours.
(Pause.)
STERN: You look tired, Stephen. Have you been sleeping?
(No response.)
Have you?
STEPHEN: Yes.
STERN: I don't believe it.
STEPHEN: I'm fine.
STERN: No you're not, you look terrible. You've been having the nightmares again, haven't you.
STEPHEN: No.
STERN: Yes you have, Stephen, you obviously have. Now why don't you tell me about them.
STEPHEN: I haven't been having—
STERN: Stephen.
STEPHEN: Honestly, there's nothing—
STERN: Stephen. I am here to help you. You know that.
STEPHEN: Yes.
STERN: Not hinder you.
STEPHEN: I know.
STERN: I love you Stephen. And Christ loves you. But we cannot help you unless you are honest with us. Unless you tell us the truth.
(Pause.)
STEPHEN: I, uh … I think I told you about a diary. Didn't I?
STERN: A diary?
STEPHEN: My father's diary. It was in the papers and I thought it didn't exist.

STERN: Oh yes. What about it.

STEPHEN: It does exist. Peter had it. And I've been reading it.

STERN: I see.

STEPHEN: Jonathan, I think we may have been wrong. About everything.

STERN: Go on.

STEPHEN: Well it's ... it describes things ... his thoughts, his feelings, page after page and it's all mixed in with scripture. *(Pause.)* He ... he used to drink a lot, he ... I never told you this. He used to shout at us, and swear ... And it was never at me, it was Peter, always at Peter, see ... see he decided that Peter was the Bad One. Peter was the Bad One and I was the Good One. That's what he called us. And I was the Good One. I mean he just *decided,* for no reason, we didn't have any choice.

STERN: You've never told me about this Stephen.

STEPHEN: I know—

STERN: Why didn't you tell me.

STEPHEN: That's just it, I ... God, somehow I forgot about it or something. I must have *repressed* it, I don't know *how,* I guess that's just what people do, right, they *repress* it. I think it's fairly common—

STERN: All right—

STEPHEN: I had the feeling that it was all a dream, that I had dreamt it. But I couldn't have dreamt it because it was all right there. In that book, it was written down. *(Pause.)* Jonathan, it's not the writing of a good man.

STERN: Well—

STEPHEN: I think we were wrong.

STERN: Just—

STEPHEN: About everything. We were *wrong*.

STERN: Well just, now, hold on a moment Stephen, just calm down. We weren't wrong. Of course we weren't. I mean ... do you think that God is wrong because He sees that every man contains goodness? Do you think that Christ is wrong because he would die for you, or your father, again, upon the cross? Do you think the Bible is wrong because it says that we are forgiven, that our sins are forgiven Stephen, that "God in Christ has forgiven us." Is that what you think?

STEPHEN: *No,* of course not, I just ...

STERN: Clearly your father was troubled, he had some problems, we all do. It doesn't mean anything. *(Pause.)* This is what I want you to do. I want you to bring this diary to me. Okay? We'll go through it, page by page, we'll see what's in it. Okay Stephen?

STEPHEN: Okay.

STERN: We'll talk about it.

STEPHEN: Okay.

STERN: As for right now ... right now you have to stop stewing about it. You have to get some sleep, you have to stay *healthy*. You mustn't let this upset you.

STEPHEN: Right.

STERN: And you mustn't let *Peter* upset you. I'm afraid this only proves my point. You're not ready to deal with your brother yet, you're not strong enough. No, Stephen, you're not. Which is why Peter must go. For your own safety. *(Pause.)* Frankly, I don't know what I was thinking. It was foolish to bring him here, I mean you're clearly in a conflict of interest on this. *(Pause.)* I think you'd better speak to him. Right away. And the committee. All right Stephen?

(No response.)

Would you rather I did it?

STEPHEN: *(Quiet.)* No. I'll do it.

STERN: You'll speak to Peter?

STEPHEN: Yes.

STERN: And the committee?

STEPHEN: Yes.

STERN: Good. Believe me, Stephen, it's for the best. *(Pause.)* Now. I want you to stop thinking about it. Okay? Just close your eyes. Just close them Stephen. Close your eyes. Are they closed? Stephen? Are they closed?

Scene Two

(A radio studio. PETER and LINDA sit across from each other, each with microphone and headphones. LINDA has a sheet of questions.)

LINDA: *(Into microphone.)* Marty? Can you hear me? *(Listens.)* Okay. Test one, two, test, test. Today we have a very special guest in the studio, a bright young pastor with a foul mouth, the Reverend— *(Breaks off, listens.)* Okay? *(Listens. Then, to PETER.)* Did you get that?

(PETER nods.)

Just say anything, he has to get a level.

PETER: *(Into microphone.)* Hello? Hello?

(LINDA gestures to keep talking.)

Uh, my name is Peter Maclean.

LINDA: Reverend.

PETER: *Reverend* Peter Maclean, right, and I think that the Bible is bull—*(Breaks off, listens.)* You're welcome.

LINDA: Okay Marty? *(To PETER.)* Okay. Are you nervous?

PETER: Yes.

LINDA: Don't be. Remember. We're gonna go back and edit.

PETER: Okay.

LINDA: So don't worry about rambling on, and above all don't censor yourself.

PETER: Okay.

LINDA: You don't look nervous.

PETER: Good.

LINDA: You look great.

(PETER smiles.)

Standby. *(Into microphone.)* Ready Marty? *(Listens.)* Here we go.

(She reads from a text.)

As long as human beings have been able to think and to reason, we have been asking the questions: What is right? What is wrong? We have been grappling with the concept of morality.

Primitive societies placed morality alongside authority and power: Might Means Right. Then, thankfully, the emphasis shifted to the spiritual. Morality became the domain of religion. Moral documents were developed, the most famous being, of course, the Christian Bible. For two thousand years the Bible has led us down the dangerous paths of morality, and, for Christians at least, it has had absolute authority. Until today. More and more Christians are asking a new question: Is the Bible always right? Can it sometimes be wrong? I'm joined in the studio today by one of those Christians. His name is Reverend Peter Maclean. Peter, hello.

PETER: Hi Linda.

LINDA: So. *Can* the Bible sometimes be wrong?

PETER: Well, I believe so, yes. *(Clears throat, refers to notes.)* For example, in Matthew fifteen verse four the Bible says, "Whoever curses his father or his mother is to be put to death."

LINDA: Whoa.

PETER: Or in Ephesians, "Wives must submit themselves completely to their husbands."

LINDA: Right.

(Without breaking the rhythm of the interview, LINDA takes Peter's notes away. PETER tries to get them back. LINDA smiles, motions PETER to keep talking.)

PETER: And that's just the beginning. Now obviously, we wouldn't consider those statements to be morally right.

LINDA: And if we question *those* verses, we're obliged to question all the other verses.

PETER: Exactly. The point being you either see the Bible as a set of guidelines or as a set of rules.

LINDA: Right. What's the difference?

PETER: Well, on the one hand you take it literally, and on the other—

(PETER stops suddenly. He is thinking hard.)

LINDA: *(Aside.)* What's wrong.

PETER: *(Aside.)* Can I take that again?

LINDA: Yes.

PETER: Can I say "fuck"?

LINDA: No. Sorry.

PETER: "Asshole?"

LINDA: Yes.

PETER: *(Into microphone.)* The difference is, you either put a child to death for calling his father an "asshole" or you don't.

LINDA: I see.

PETER: Guidelines you can choose to ignore.

LINDA: Right.

PETER: You follow them in *spirit*, not in fact. You place them in their context and, sometimes, disregard them entirely. I mean, I have called my father things much worse than "asshole." And I may have been wrong to do so, but at least I'm still alive.

(LINDA laughs.)

(Aside.) You can take that or leave it.

LINDA: *(Aside.)* It's good, I'll take it. *(Into microphone.)* Okay Peter, cursing your father is one thing, but there are larger issues than that. Aren't there.

PETER: Yes.

LINDA: Such as homosexuality. Which is *the* big moral issue in the church today, and which I believe the Bible clearly condemns.

PETER: It condemns it, yes, but—

LINDA: Another guideline to be followed in spirit Peter?

PETER: Well—

LINDA: Because other ministers in your church would say that on this point the Bible must be obeyed.

PETER: Really?

LINDA: *Yes,* they use Bible verses to justify the *repression* of homosexuals, to—

PETER: Which ones.

LINDA: Which verses?

PETER: No, which ministers.

(LINDA smiles.)

I'm new in town.

LINDA: Well, for example, Reverend Jonathan Stern.

PETER: He's at St. Andrew's isn't he?

LINDA: *(Smiling.)* Yes, actually, he is.

PETER: What verses *did* he use? Leviticus?

LINDA: *(Referring to notes.)* Leviticus, Genesis, Corinthians—

PETER: Right, the same tired old scripture, I've heard it a hundred times. Okay. Let's talk about context. Reverend Stern quotes Leviticus: "No man is to have sexual relations with another man ... it is an abomination." Fine. But what he doesn't tell us is that a page or so later, Leviticus also says, "Both men shall be put to death."

LINDA: Right.

PETER: What he *doesn't* tell us is that the Hebrew word for "abomination" is the same word used to describe menstruating women! The Biblical writers were afraid of menstruation. They were afraid of homosexuality!

LINDA: Really.

PETER: *(Enjoying himself.)* My question is, how can Jonathan Stern tell us that one verse is valid, and the other isn't. Who gave him that power?

LINDA: Good question.

PETER: By taking a pair of scissors and *snipping* these Bible verses out of context, by *editing,* he's clearly exercising a bias, he's using the Bible to legitimize his personal hatred, all because of fear. I mean, here he is, he's living thousands of years after Leviticus was written. He's managed to overcome his fear of *menstruation,* why hasn't he overcome his fear of homosexuality?

(LINDA laughs.)

I mean, here's a guy, he gets up into the pulpit every Sunday and spews *poison,* he, he uses the Bible to *terrorize* the minds and souls of his congregation! And he's going to define our morality? I don't think so.

LINDA: *(Aside.)* Peter, I can't use this.

PETER: *(Aside.)* Sure you can, come on, it's great, it's provocative.

LINDA: *(Aside.)* It's *slander!*

PETER: *(Into microphone.)* I mean, frankly Linda, I consider Stern to be a villain, I do, he's like the devil. He's like—he's like, um ... Hitler. Stalin. Attila the Hun.

LINDA: *(Playing along.)* Oh yeah? So who are *you* then.

PETER: Ghandi.

LINDA: Yes.

PETER: No, Mother Theresa. Whatever.

LINDA: The good guy.

PETER: Right.

LINDA: And Stern's the bad guy. Look, Peter, we're wasting tape. Let's get back on track okay? *(Into microphone.)* Hang in there Marty. *(To*

PETER.) This is good though, don't get me wrong, you're being very, you know ... uncensored.

(PETER says nothing.)

Are you okay?

PETER: Yes.

LINDA: What. What is it.

PETER: Nothing.

LINDA: What's wrong.

PETER: I'm fine.

LINDA: *(Beat.)* Okay. Well then let's change the subject. *(Into microphone.)* Peter, I understand your father was also a minister. A rather notorious minister—

PETER: *(Interrupting, aside.)* Wait. Can I just say one more thing about Stern?

LINDA: Okay.

PETER: *(Into microphone.)* Ministers like Jonathan Stern, and the poison they preach, are incredibly destructive Linda, to all of society. But, of course, they are especially destructive to homosexuals. Like me.

LINDA: What?

PETER: As a gay minister I can personally attest to the damage that Stern is doing. But I will not *let* him destroy me.

LINDA: Peter—

PETER: I challenge Reverend Stern to look me in the eye, and tell me that I am unfit to be a minister of Christ.

LINDA: *(Aside.)* What are you doing?

PETER: *(Aside.)* You told me not to censor myself.

LINDA: I know, but—

PETER: So I'm not.

LINDA: But you're not gay.

PETER: Yes, but your listeners don't know that.

LINDA: What?

PETER: Come on, let's try it, let's see where it goes.

LINDA: No way. Forget it.

Castrato 61

PETER: Why not? This is good, it's more direct, it's, it's *concrete,* it's a specific *context—*

LINDA: *No.*

PETER: Why not?

LINDA: *Because,* the whole point is that you *aren't* gay—

PETER: *(Overlapping.)* No—

LINDA: —and yet you are still *affected—*

PETER: No, listen, we need a *context—*

LINDA: Peter! Stop it, we don't need a context! *(Pause.)* Look. Just let me do this all right? Trust me. I know what I'm doing. Let's talk about your father.

PETER: *(Into microphone.)* Sorry, I'd rather not talk about him.

LINDA: *(Beat.)* All right. Your sermon then, the castration metaphor.

PETER: No, I don't want to talk about that either. Sorry.

(Pause.)

LINDA: *(Into microphone.)* Marty could you stop the tape please. I need a couple of minutes. Thank you.

(LINDA takes her headphones off. PETER does too.)

PETER: I have an idea. Okay, so, I'm a young minister, I'm up for a job at the biggest church in the city, right, Jonathan *Stern's* church. So I preach a couple of sermons, I sign a contract, I get the job. *Then* we broadcast this interview. And it turns out I'm gay.

LINDA: No.

PETER: Just, listen. So I'm gay. So they of course drop me like a hot potato, *but,* I have a *contract,* right? So, I charge them with discrimination, you interview me again, and now we have an actual *case,* now we're not just *talking* about it.

LINDA: Are you crazy?

PETER: It's perfect! It allows us to pull this issue out of the church, which must be done, and place it in the public eye.

LINDA: No way.

PETER: Why *not?* Come on, it's a great story.

LINDA: It is *not* a great story. *You* are a great story, I *told* you that.

PETER: No I'm not. I have no authority. If I'm straight my entire argument is academic. If I'm gay I have authority.

LINDA: That's ridiculous.

PETER: I thought you wanted to make people think.

LINDA: I *do*, but this won't work. It's sensational, *and*, it's a pack of lies!

PETER: Well—

LINDA: When they find out you're straight, you'll lose *all* credibility, and so will *real* homosexuals.

PETER: No, because we'll come clean. We'll say we did it to make a point.

LINDA: And then *I'll* lose credibility.

PETER: Okay, then we'll say you didn't know, that I fooled you too. I mean, how could you possibly have known I wasn't gay?

(Pause.)

LINDA: This is getting to be a habit with you.

PETER: What.

LINDA: Lying in interviews.

PETER: What do you mean.

LINDA: Next thing you'll be saying is Stern goes to prostitutes.

PETER: *(Beat.)* What?

LINDA: It's the same thing! How is it different?

PETER: It *is* dif—

LINDA: No it isn't! You can't be the Traumatized Teenage Son anymore so you have to be the Traumatized Gay Minister. Well stop it, you're not a victim. *(Pause.)* Look, maybe twelve years ago they weren't concerned with the truth. But I am.

PETER: Oh, please.

LINDA: What?

PETER: You're no different Linda, you said it yourself, all you want is a good story.

LINDA: Peter—

PETER: Don't be a hypocrite.

LINDA: What?

PETER: I said, don't be a hypocrite.

(Pause.)

LINDA: What are you doing. Are you sulking? Because I don't like your idea? *(Pause.)* Look, let's just get back to the interview, okay? We were talking about your—

PETER: No. There's no point *talking* about morality. It must be supported by action, otherwise it is immoral.

LINDA: Peter—

PETER: I am interested in action.

LINDA: You are acting, Peter, you're getting the job. Remember? That's action. Now don't screw it up. *(Pause.)* Where is this coming from? Are you frightened, is that it?

PETER: Of course not.

LINDA: There's nothing to be frightened of.

PETER: I'm not frightened.

Scene Three

(PETER and STEPHEN are in Peter's hotel room. PETER is typing on a lap-top computer. STEPHEN has the diary.)

STEPHEN: I've been trying to call you. Did you get my messages?

PETER: No.

STEPHEN: I've been leaving messages, why didn't you get them?

PETER: I don't know.

STEPHEN: Have you spoken to Jonathan?

PETER: No.

STEPHEN: You haven't been in to the church?

PETER: No, I've been working here.

STEPHEN: Good. What are you writing, is that your sermon?

PETER: Yes.

STEPHEN: We have to talk about that.

PETER: Why.

STEPHEN: Because ... Jonathan's called it off.

PETER: What?

STEPHEN: He's upset about the other day, about what you said, and ... and he's not going to let you preach again. *(Pause.)* I'm sorry, Peter, I tried to tell him he was overreacting, but he's just very angry and he wouldn't listen—

PETER: Stephen we've been through this—

STEPHEN: I know—

PETER: It's not Stern's decision—

STEPHEN: Well, actually, that's not exactly true. I misjudged his influence on the committee. I'm sorry Peter, I screwed up on this.

PETER: You said—

STEPHEN: I know what I said and I was wrong. Okay? I was wrong. *(Pause.)* But it's not that big a deal. We don't have to give up yet. I know the committee likes you, all right, you've made a good impression there ... so, if you apologize to Jonathan, if, if we let him cool off a bit, a couple of weeks, maybe a month, and if I talk to him, then ... I'm sure he'll let you come back, I'm sure of it. All right? So don't panic. It's not over yet.

PETER: *(Pause.)* You want me to apologize.

STEPHEN: Yes.

PETER: To Jonathan.

STEPHEN: Yes. For being rude.

PETER: *(Pause.)* What exactly is his influence?

STEPHEN: Well, the committee members respect his opinion. He hasn't said anything yet ... but he will.

PETER: Unless I leave town.

STEPHEN: Unless you apologize. And let him cool off.

PETER: You realize it's illegal.

STEPHEN: It's not *illegal,* it's ... it's just how these things work.

PETER: No, actually, it's illegal.

STEPHEN: Peter—

PETER: I don't believe you. I don't think he *does* control the committee.

STEPHEN: What?

PETER: I think he controls you. *(Pause.)* And I think you have to make a choice. Because you can't have it both ways. Stern and I don't go together, Stephen. We're incompatible.

STEPHEN: Look—

PETER: I'm not going to apologize. And I'm not coming back in a couple of weeks. So make your choice.

STEPHEN: Peter, it's not that simple.

Castrato 65

PETER: Yes it—
STEPHEN: No it isn't! You obviously don't understand how these things work. This is not a perfect world designed to suit you personally, you have to be willing to *work* with people, to give and take, to, to—
PETER: Compromise.
STEPHEN: *No,* not compromise, *no.* You simply have to be open, you have to be ... well, fair!
PETER: You think I'm being unfair?
STEPHEN: Yes, frankly, I do. I think you are being unfair to Jonathan, and I think you are being unfair to our father.
PETER: What?
STEPHEN: You—
PETER: Our father?
STEPHEN: You act like—
PETER: Our father has nothing to do with it.
STEPHEN: *(Angry.)* Of course he does! God, you act like some kind of *martyr,* like your suffering has made you holy, has taken you to some higher place, some holy pulpit, where you can look down on us and *judge.*
PETER: Stephen.
STEPHEN: You're not the only one who suffered!!
   (Pause.)
PETER: What are we talking about here Stephen. We're not talking about this job. Are we. Because this job and our father are separate issues. They're separate.
   (No response.)
You've been reading the diary.
STEPHEN: Yes.
PETER: And you still think I should forgive him?
   (No response.)
You still think he was a good man? That he was "troubled"?
STEPHEN: Look, I agree there's some bad stuff in here, no question. But that doesn't prove anything. I mean in places it reads like it was written by ...

PETER: By who.

STEPHEN: Well, by someone in pain! By someone *human* who was, who was in *conflict,* who *hated* himself, who needed *help!*

PETER: What?

STEPHEN: I mean you can't read this and then just write him off completely, no you *can't!* What about his faith? He was wrestling with demons—

PETER: Oh come on—

STEPHEN: He was! He was *tormented!* He was struggling with his faith, and, and the *Bible*—

PETER: He was *using* the Bible—

STEPHEN: No!

PETER: He cut it to pieces.

STEPHEN: No, he wasn't *using* it, he was pleading with it, he was begging for ... for something, I don't know what—

PETER: Stephen, he destroyed me! He wore me down, bit by bit, methodically, he *erased* me! There was nothing human about it!

(Pause.)

I remember the day he died. I remember sitting in church, watching him preach. And he was really into it, he was shouting and waving his arms, and his face was all purple from the strain and then suddenly, *suddenly,* he stopped. In mid-rant. It was ... it was like he just ... collapsed. His face caved in. And then he looked at me. He looked right at me, *directly* at me and he said, "You have castrated me." Now you tell me. What was he begging for. *Huh?*

(STEPHEN says nothing.)

Look, you're not going to change what I think, all right, you're not going to "help" me, it's not going to happen. So give it up.

(Pause.)

STEPHEN: I don't know. Maybe he was begging for a miracle. Maybe he was broken and he was begging for someone to put him back together.

(Pause.)

I have a lot of nightmares. I always have, they keep me awake, it's nothing new. Most of them are about the suicide, and about leaving, and seeing your face as I drive away. But lately I've been having a new one.

In it I'm a child, I'm about ... twelve. I'm lying in bed at night. Upstairs. Lying awake, listening. He's downstairs. The TV's on but he's not watching it. He's talking to himself. Sometimes singing. I can't make out the words.

After a while the talking gets louder. It becomes shouting. He starts slamming doors, things start rattling in my room. At this point I'm not scared yet. I'm just lying there. But then I hear your name. Then he starts screaming your name. Over and over. And I know he's standing there, I picture him, at the bottom of the stairs, screaming your name.

And then I hear you. Opening your door ... walking down the hall ... towards the stairs ... and then the shouting stops because he's seen you ...

And then I wake up.

That's it. It doesn't sound like much, does it. But it keeps me awake.

(Pause.)

Now, if I was to analyze that dream I would have to say that ... that it comes from a very strong sense of guilt.

PETER: Guilt?

STEPHEN: Yes.

PETER: Guilt for what?

STEPHEN: For being good.

(PETER looks at him.)

For being the Good One.

PETER: That's crazy.

STEPHEN: No, it isn't. You don't understand. Because I was bad, that's just it. That's what makes it worse—

PETER: Wait—

STEPHEN: *(Picks up diary.)* I mean when I was reading this it was ... it was like this man was me. It was like *I* had done these things, not him.

PETER: Look—

STEPHEN: Don't you get it!? I was the good one! If I wasn't good, you wouldn't've been bad!

PETER: No.

STEPHEN: I let it happen! I lay in my bed and I shut my ears! And I closed my eyes! And I pretended to be asleep! I am a sinner, Peter, God help me, I have sinned!

PETER: Stephen!

STEPHEN: And I cannot forgive myself! I *need* you, Peter, I ... I need your forgiveness, I need you to say that I *am* good, I *am,* I need you to save my *life!* I need you to, I need ...

I need ...

I need ...

(Pause.)

PETER: What a crock of shit. Who says you're a sinner? Stern? Did he tell you that?

(No response.)

(Intense.) Listen to me. You don't need my forgiveness. Because you didn't do anything *wrong*. *(Pause.)* Don't you see what's happening? You're being manipulated Stephen, Stern is using you. To hurt me. Exactly like our father did.

(STEPHEN looks up, looks at him.)

If you want to be a sinner, go ahead, go and feel *guilty*, go and ... and *wank* with Stern. But don't include me. Because I think it's pathetic. *(Pause.)* I want you to tell him something. From me. Tell him it's not going to work. I agreed to preach two sermons. And that's what I intend to do. You tell him that. Okay? Stephen?

Scene Four

(STERN, preaching. He holds a Bible, waves it about from time to time. He doesn't preach from a text. His style is grand, emotional.)

STERN: "The law is laid down not for the innocent but for the lawless and disobedient, for the godless and sinful, for the unholy and profane, for those who kill their father or mother, for murderers, fornicators, for sodomites ... and whatever else is contrary to the sound teaching of the glorious gospel of the blessed God ..."

"... the glorious gospel of the blessed God ..."

(He pauses.)

You know, I can't help thinking, as I stand up here this morning and look down upon you ... I can't help thinking what good people you are. Good solid people, struggling to live your lives the best way you know how. Making *decisions* the best way you know how. Raising your *children* the best way you know how. Loving your *wives* and *husbands* the best way you know how. Looking out from your lives upon the world, looking at the world, seeing the darkness in the world, the tragedies, the sorrow, the *indecencies,* looking at these things and, though you are overcome by the shamefulness of this world, you lift your heads, and you march into it, and you embrace it, and you *live* in it ... the best way you know how.

Or do you?

My question to you this morning, my question is ... are you doing enough? Are you conquering the darkness? Or are you advancing it? Are you like those of whom Paul speaks in his letter to the Romans, those who, though they knew God, did not honour him, or give thanks to him, but whose minds were darkened, who exchanged the truth of God for a lie, who gave themselves up, in the lusts of their hearts, to impurity ...

Are you like these? I think not. I *pray* not. I pray that you know better.

(He allows his rage to build.)

For I can tell you, I am here this morning to tell you, that we are no longer ignorant! We *have* the knowledge of good and evil. Eve gave us that knowledge! When she took the apple she cursed us with that knowledge! With the *responsibility* of that knowledge! The Bible gives us guidance. We must be strong, we must be ruthless in our efforts to find evil and halt it in it's tracks!

(STERN is interrupted by PETER, shouting from the back of the church. Bright television camera lights are turned on, making STERN squint. PETER moves to the front of the church. He has his sermon in one hand, a Bible in the other.)

PETER: "Love God and do as you please!"

STERN: What?

PETER: "Love God and do as you please!" The words of St. Augustine! "Love God and do as you please!"

(PETER reads from his sermon.)

I'm not going to give a scripture lesson. I'm sick of the Bible. Read it yourself. *(Puts Bible down.)*

STERN: Reverend Maclean—

PETER: Please don't be alarmed or distracted by the television lights. Unfortunately, they are necessary.

STERN: All right Reverend—

PETER: Now. I've told you about the Castrati. But what I didn't tell you is that at the end of a performance, members of the astonished audience often cried out "Long Live the Knife!" as a kind of grotesque tribute.

STERN: Peter!

PETER: "Long Live the Knife"? Obviously the Castrati were as much victims of a bloodthirsty society as they were of the bloodthirsty bishops—

(STERN takes Peter's sermon, crumples the sheets of paper.)

STERN: STOP IT!

(PETER tries to get sermon back, fails.)

That's *enough*. *(To television cameras.)* Turn those lights off immediately! *(The lights stay on. STERN addresses the congregation.)* Please excuse this interruption—

PETER: *(To congregation.)* No! Don't listen to this man! He is perverting the Bible, he is preaching hatred and, and intolerance.

STERN: Peter—

PETER: And he wants *you* to be hateful, and he wants *you* to be intolerant. *(To STERN.)* Tell me something, Reverend Stern. Why do you refuse to let me speak? *(To congregation.)* I was supposed to preach to you again today. I had an agreement with the search committee of your church—

STERN: Peter—

PETER: But this man said no! This man intervened, this man over-rode the democratic process! He would not let me speak! For one reason! For one reason! Because I am gay!

STERN: What?

PETER: Because I am a gay minister! He would not let me speak!

(STERN just looks at him. PETER plunges on.)

He thinks that homosexual love is wrong, that it is *evil*, that gays must not be ordained! But *he* is wrong! I challenge you Reverend Stern! I challenge you to look me in the eye and tell me that I am evil! That I am bad! That I am unfit to be a Minister of Christ!

(STERN says nothing. PETER turns, triumphant, to the congregation.)

Castrato 71

This man is the bloodthirsty bishop! He has performed an act of castration! And you—you are the blood-thirsty audience, listen to yourselves, you are shouting "Long Live The Knife!" And look at me! I stand here before you this morning, and I am castrated! Yes! Look at me! Look me in the eye! I am castrated! This man has castrated me! And *you* have castrated me! You have castrated ... you have ... *(He falters.)* I am ... I am ...

(Sudden silence. PETER very still.)

STERN: You are who, Peter?

PETER: *No! Listen to me! Listen to me!*

STERN: We're listening, Peter. All of us are listening.

(PETER says nothing.)

Sit down Peter. Go and sit down.

(STERN hands PETER the crumpled sermon. PETER takes it and exits. STERN pauses, looks out at his congregation, squinting in the television lights.)

(To congregation.) My apologies. I'm sorry you had to see that. But, in a way, I'm glad that it happened. Peter Maclean is a troubled man. It is he that St. Paul is speaking of: he whose mind is darkened ... he who has exchanged the truth of God for a lie. We must pray for him. We must pray that he may open his heart, that he may yet receive God's mercy. Come ... let us pray.

Scene Five

(The sanctuary of St. Andrew's. PETER is alone. He kneels, head down. Beside him is the crumpled sermon.

LINDA enters.)

LINDA: There you are, where have you been?

PETER: Hiding.

LINDA: Everyone was looking for you.

PETER: I was downstairs. In the boiler room.

LINDA: Are you okay?

PETER: Yes.

(Pause. They look at each other.)

LINDA: That was absurd.

PETER: I know.

LINDA: That was completely ridiculous.
PETER: I know.
LINDA: What did you possibly think you'd accomplish.
PETER: I don't know.
LINDA: I mean there were cameras here! In a church! Where did the cameras come from?
PETER: I invited them.
LINDA: What?
PETER: I said, I invited them to come.
LINDA: Why?
PETER: Because I was determined to make a fool of myself. And you wouldn't let me, and Stern wouldn't let me. So I sent out a press release. And they came.
LINDA: You're kidding.
PETER: I know, it was ridiculous, I know that.
LINDA: *(Pause.)* Well you certainly made it worth their while.
PETER: What do you mean.
LINDA: I mean it was pretty spectacular. They're gonna love it. Obviously I was right.
PETER: About what.
LINDA: About you being a good story.
PETER: Yeah.
LINDA: Who knows, you might even make the national news.
PETER: Just like my father did?
LINDA: *(Beat.)* Yeah. Just like your father.
   (Pause.)
   It was fear, wasn't it. You were terrified.
PETER: Yes.
LINDA: You were running scared.
PETER: It was a nightmare. A bad dream. *(Pause.)* I could hear my father's words pounding through my head. And then I realized that I wasn't dreaming. Then the voice changed and became my voice, and suddenly the words were coming out of my mouth. And then I felt the fear. Rushing up from inside. And I finally discovered where the evil

was. Why I felt afraid. It was within me. *(Pause.)* I think I just committed suicide.

LINDA: I don't. I think you just woke up.

(PETER looks at her.)

Are you screaming? Are you?

PETER: No.

LINDA: Why not? What's giving you the strength not to scream?

(No response.)

I think you were wrong Peter. I don't think fear is the rational response to evil. I think it's the rational response to being alive.

(Pause. PETER looks at her.

STEPHEN enters.)

STEPHEN: There you are.

PETER: Hi Stephen.

STEPHEN: I've been looking for you everywhere, I thought you left.

LINDA: He was in the boiler room.

STEPHEN: What?

PETER: Stephen this is Linda Clark. Linda, Stephen Maclean. My brother.

STEPHEN: Hi.

LINDA: Hello.

PETER: Linda's a radio journalist.

STEPHEN: She is?

PETER: It's okay, she's off duty.

LINDA: That's right. I'm safe.

PETER: Where's Stern, I've been expecting him.

STEPHEN: I don't know, he was out front. Talking to the reporters. He was giving them a statement.

PETER: Oh.

STEPHEN: Yeah.

LINDA: Uh, listen, I should go. I'll ... I'll go see what's happening. I know some of them, maybe I can talk them out of it. Maybe. I doubt it. *(To PETER.)* Look. Today isn't a disaster. All right? It might even be a victory. I'll see you later.

(LINDA begins to exit.)
PETER: Linda, wait.
(LINDA stops.)
Listen ...
LINDA: Peter. I'll see you later, okay? Promise.
PETER: I'll call you.
LINDA: Great. Bye.
(She exits. PETER and STEPHEN look at each other.)
STEPHEN: Are you okay?
PETER: Yeah. I'm sorry Stephen.
STEPHEN: Me too.
PETER: That was unforgivable.
STEPHEN: No. Don't feel that way. Listen, I was wrong—
PETER: No—
STEPHEN: About everything, I ... I—
PETER: Stephen—
STEPHEN: I could see you. *(Pause.)* In that moment when you ... when you cracked open. I could see things, Peter ... I could see you.
(STERN enters. He is angry, but determined not to be.)
STERN: Ah hah. There you are. Peter, I'd like to speak to you in my office please.
PETER: You can speak to me here.
STERN: Well, I'd rather—
PETER: If you don't mind.
STEPHEN: I don't think it's necessary Jonathan. You can speak to Peter here.
STERN: *(Pause.)* All right. I've just been dealing with the reporters.
PETER: What did you tell them.
STERN: Well, Peter, I apologized. For you. For wasting their time.
PETER: And what did they say.
STERN: They said they're going to put you on the news. Tonight.
PETER: Oh.
STERN: Peter I don't know what kind of behaviour you think is appropriate for a minister of—

PETER: Please. Don't bother.

STERN: Sorry?

PETER: Save the big speech. I really don't want to hear it right now.

STERN: *(Pause.)* All right. Well then I'll simply say that in my opinion Peter you are lacking sufficient gifts. For ministry. And I intend to propose that presbytery strike a review committee.

STEPHEN: What?

STERN: And I intend to propose to that committee that your license be revoked. I'm sorry Peter.

STEPHEN: Jonathan, that isn't necessary.

STERN: I'm afraid it is.

STEPHEN: No. It isn't. And frankly I don't think that you should talk about committees.

STERN: What do you mean.

STEPHEN: I mean that—that maybe I should call presbytery. And maybe I should tell them how search committees work here at St. Andrews.

STERN: *(Pause.)* Well Stephen, you can do what you like. I'm sure they'll be fascinated to hear that the chairman and the applicant are, in fact, brothers.

(No response.)

I am not the villain here, Stephen. I have been trying to help.

(He turns to PETER.)

I'm sorry that things have turned out this way Peter, I truly am. Perhaps if you had told me from the start that you were ... homosexual, this whole thing could have been- -

PETER: I'm not gay.

STERN: What?

PETER: I'm not gay.

STEPHEN: You're not?

PETER: No. I was lying.

(Pause. This has shattered STERN's determined patience.)

STERN: Tell me Peter. How did you become a minister? You seem to have no concept of what it means. That there are people who *listen* to you when you speak. You're not actually aware of your congregation are you Peter, you don't actually *see* them. I think you think you're on television. All you're aware of is what goes on inside your own head. That box on top of your neck.

>   *(He pauses. He is very angry.)*

Let me tell you what I believe. I believe in a loving God. I believe that Jesus Christ died for us upon a cross, that our sins may be *forgiven*. I believe that if we, as human beings, can summon up the courage and the *humility* to kneel before our God and accept this love, that we may yet survive. As a species. That we might find the strength, in turn, to love each other. That is what I believe.

Now tell me Peter. What do you believe?

>   *(STERN is looking at PETER. PETER looks down.)*

I am going to my office. If either of you would like to talk, please, come and see me. My door is always open.

>   *(STERN turns abruptly and exits.)*

STEPHEN: You're not giving up. We're gonna fight this.

PETER: No—

STEPHEN: *(Pointing after STERN.)* That is *bullshit,* listen, I can, I'll talk to presbytery—

PETER: *No.*

STEPHEN: We can't just let him *do* that! You're not going to lose your license.

PETER: Maybe I should.

STEPHEN: No you *shouldn't.*

PETER: I'm too fucked up to be a minister.

STEPHEN: No, you're *not* Peter, I mean ... I mean that's what *qualifies* you, isn't it? That's ... I mean who *isn't?*

PETER: Stephen—

STEPHEN: You're not giving up! *(Pause.)* I'm sorry. I'm ... I just ... I thought you were great up there.

PETER: What?

STEPHEN: I *did,* it doesn't matter what you said, I could *see* you. I could ... I could feel what you were feeling, and ... and it felt so ... *familiar.*

PETER: It did?

STEPHEN: *Yes.* It *did.*

(PETER looks at STEPHEN.)
PETER: You were right Stephen.
STEPHEN: What.
PETER: You and Jonathan. I need help.
STEPHEN: *(Smiles.)* Yeah. Me too.
PETER: I think we should talk.
STEPHEN: You do?
PETER: Why didn't we talk yet?
STEPHEN: I don't know.
PETER: I mean ... it's been twelve years.
STEPHEN: I know.
PETER: We should have talked.
STEPHEN: That's right.
PETER: I think he wasn't evil. Dad. I think he was just ...
STEPHEN: What.
PETER: ... fucked up.
STEPHEN: *(Pause.)* Maybe. But that doesn't change the bottom line.
PETER: Which is what.
STEPHEN: That he was also a bastard.
(Pause. PETER smiles.)
Am I right?
PETER: Yeah.
STEPHEN: He was also a son of a bitch.
(They smile.)
Come on. Let's get out of here, this place is getting on my nerves.
PETER: You go ahead. I'll be right there.
STEPHEN: Why. What do you have to do?
PETER: Just give me a minute.
STEPHEN: *(Pause.)* Okay. But don't be long.
PETER: I won't.
STEPHEN: I'll be in the car.
PETER: Okay.
STEPHEN: It's parked round the back.

PETER: Okay.

STEPHEN: I'll be ... I'll be waiting.

   (STEPHEN exits.

   PETER picks up his crumpled sermon. He moves to the pulpit, retrieves his Bible.

   Then he is still, standing alone in the pulpit.)

PETER: I believe ...

  I believe ...

  I believe ...

   (He is unable to finish.

   He stands, still, struggling.

   End of play.)

Plays available from Blizzard Publishing

- *Amigo's Blue Guitar*, MacLeod, J.
  $10.95 (pb) 0-921368-23-2
- *Beautiful Lake Winnipeg*, Hunter, M.
  $10.95 (pb) 0-921368-10-0
- *Bordertown Café*, Rebar, K.
  $10.95 (pb) 0-921368-08-9
- *Castrato*, Nelson, G.
  $11.95 (pb) 0-921368-31-3
- *Chinese Man Said Goodbye, The*, McManus, B.
  $10.95 (pb) 0-921368-05-4
- *Darling Family, The: A Duet for Three*, Griffiths, L.
  $10.95 (pb) 0-921368-17-8
- *Democracy*, Murrell, J.
  $10.95 (pb) 0-921368-28-3
- *Departures and Arrivals*, Shields, C.
  $10.95 (pb) 0-921368-13-5
- *Exile*, Crail, A.
  $10.95 (pb) 0-921368-12-7
- *Fire*, Ledoux, P. & Young, D.
  $9.95 (pb) 0-929091-05-1
- *Footprints On the Moon*, Hunter, M.
  $10.95 (pb) 0-921368-07-0
- *Gravel Run*, Massing, C.
  $10.95 (pb) 0-921368-16-X
- *Invention of Poetry, The*, Quarrington, P.
  $9.95 (pb) 0-929091-31-0
- *Mail Order Bride, The*, Clinton, R.
  $10.95 (pb) 0-921368-09-7
- *Memories of You*, Lill, W.
  $9.95 (pb) 0-929091-06-X
- *Midnight Madness*, Carley, D.
  $9.95 (pb) 0-920197-88-4
- *Mirror Game*, Foon, D.
  $10.95 (pb) 0-921368-24-0
- *Oldest Living, The*, Smith, P.
  $5.95 (pb) 0-920999-02-6
- *Particular Class of Women, A*, Feindel, J.
  $7.95 (pb) 0-920999-10-7
- *Prairie Report*, Moher, F.
  $10.95 (pb) 0-921368-15-1
- *refugees*, Rintoul, H.
  $7.95 (pb) 0-921368-02-X
- *Sky*, Gault, C.
  $10.95 (pb) 0-921368-06-2
- *Soft Eclipse, The*, Gault, C.
  $10.95 (pb) 0-921368-14-3
- *Steel Kiss*, Fulford, R.
  $10.95 (pb) 0-921368-19-4
- *Stillborn Lover, The*, Findley, T.
  $15.95 (hc) 0-921368-33-X
- *Third Ascent, The*, Moher, F.
  $10.95 (pb) 0-921368-04-6
- *Thirteen Hands*, Shields, C.
  $11.95 (pb) 0-921368-30-5
- *Transit of Venus*, Hunter, M.
  $10.95 (pb) 0-921368-29-1
- *Unidentified Human Remains and the True Nature of Love*, Fraser, B.
  $10.95 (pb) 0-921368-11-9
- *Writing With Our Feet*, Carley, D.
  $10.95 (pb) 0-921368-20-8

Anthologies

- *Adventures for (Big) Girls: Seven Radio Plays*, Jansen, A. (Ed.)
  $16.95 (pb) 0-921368-32-1
- *Airborne: Radio Plays by Women*, Jansen, A. (Ed.)
  $14.95 (pb) 0-921368-22-4
- *Dangerous Traditions: A Passe Muraille Anthology*, Rudakoff, J. (Ed.)
  $19.95 (pb) 0-921368-27-5
- *Endangered Species: Four Plays*, Hollingsworth, M.
  $10.95 (pb) 0-9693639-0-1

Anthologies (cont.)

- On the MAP: Scenes Workshopped by the Manitoba Playwrights Development Program, Runnells, R. (Ed.)
$11.95 (pb) 0-9693890-0-0

- Take Five: The Morningside Dramas, Carley, D. (Ed.)
$14.95 (pb) 0-921368-21-6

Theatre Studies

- Dramatic Body, The: A Guide to Physical Characterization, Jetsmark, T. (trans. P. Brask)
$15.95 (pb) 0-921368-25-9

- Hot-Ice: Shakespeare in Moscow, A Director's Diary, Sprung, G. (with R. Much)
$15.95 (pb) 0-921368-18-6

- Women on the Canadian Stage: The Legacy of Hrotsvit, Much, R. (Ed.)
$16.95 (pb) 0-921368-26-7

To Order:

BLIZZARD PUBLISHING
301 - 89 Princess St., Winnipeg, MB
CANADA R3B 1K6

Please send me the titles I have indicated:

Name: ....

Address: ....

City: .... State/Prov.: .... Code: ....

Please send cheque or money order; no cash or C.O.D.
Add $1.50 for shipping; or 50¢ per book for orders of more than five books. Canadian residents add 7% GST. Allow three weeks for delivery.

- Free catalogues available on request.